A Murder of
Crows

By Greg Roza

Gareth Stevens
Publishing

Please visit our website, www.garethstevens.com. For a free color catalog of all our high-quality books, call toll free 1-800-542-2595 or fax 1-877-542-2596.

Library of Congress Cataloging-in-Publication Data

Roza, Greg.
 A murder of crows / Greg Roza.
    p. cm. — (Animal groups)
 Includes index.
 ISBN 978-1-4339-8205-7 (pbk.)
 ISBN 978-1-4339-8206-4 (6-pack)
 ISBN 978-1-4339-8204-0 (library binding)
 1. Crows—Juvenile literature. I. Title.
 QL696.P2367R69 2013
 598.8′64—dc23
                                        2012020375

First Edition

Published in 2013 by
Gareth Stevens Publishing
111 East 14th Street, Suite 349
New York, NY 10003

Designer: Ben Gardner
Editor: Greg Roza

3 6830 00101 5740

Photo credits: Cover, p. 1 © iStockphoto.com/tpuerzer; interior backgrounds Daniiel/Shutterstock.com; p. 5 Vlad Siaber/Shutterstock.com; p. 7 mmm/Shutterstock.com; p. 9 © iStockphoto.com/Alexsey; p. 11 jmatzick/Shutterstock.com; p. 13 Alexander Chelmodeev/Shutterstock.com; p. 15 perlphoto/Shutterstock.com; p. 17 Johann Schumacher/Peter Arnold/Getty Images; p. 19 Cheyenne Glasgow/Flickr/Getty Images; p. 21 © iStockphoto.com/Andrew Howe.

Printed in the United States of America

CPSIA compliance information: Batch #CW13GS: For further information contact Gareth Stevens, New York, New York at 1-800-542-2595.

Contents

Boldface words appear in the glossary.

Cool Bird, Creepy Name

Crows are black birds that live almost everywhere in the world. A group of crows is called a **murder**. This is because they have long been linked with death and other bad things. However, most old stories about crows are untrue.

That's a Lot of Crows!

Like other birds, crows often gather together in trees to sleep. This is called roosting. A roosting murder of crows might have 100 birds. Then again, a murder might have hundreds of thousands of crows!

7

Let's Get Together

Crows form murders for several reasons. They roost together to stay safe from enemies, such as owls. They sometimes search for food together. Most crows stay near their homes all year. However, crows that **migrate** often travel in large groups.

All in the Family

Crows often stay with the same **mate** for life. Most females lay about five eggs once a year. Parents take good care of their babies. They'll even chase away animals and people who come too close to the nest.

11

Young crows may stay with their parents for up to 7 years. They help build nests, raise baby crows, and guard family feeding sites. In time, crows leave their family to start a family of their own.

Crow Communication

Crows make noises called caws. They **communicate** using different caws. Caws can be loud, soft, long, or short. Some crows can even copy the sounds of other animals, including people. Crows use these sounds to say a lot!

Bird Brains

Scientists have discovered that crows are really smart. They learn from each other by communicating. If a crow gets into trouble, it will tell other crows so they don't make the same mistake.

17

Crows Never Forget a Face

If a person tries to hurt a crow, the bird will remember their face. It tells other crows, too. If that person comes back, the crows caw to warn each other. Parent crows even teach their young about people who are unsafe.

Playful Crows

Crows are playful. Adults sometimes do tricks while flying. Young crows in a murder sometimes play tug-of-war with sticks, stones, and cans. Some crows have even been known to steal things from people, such as keys!

Fun Facts About Crows

In the 1970s, many people believed that a crow roost in Fort Cobb, Oklahoma, had over 2 **million** crows.

Scientists think crows live about 20 years. The oldest known crow was nearly 30 years old.

One type of crow knows how to use tools! They make hooks out of sticks to pull bugs out of holes.

Glossary

communicate: to share ideas through sounds or motions

mate: one of two animals that come together to produce babies

migrate: to move to warmer or colder places for a season

million: a thousand thousands, or 1,000,000

murder: the crime of killing someone

scientist: someone who studies the way things work and the way things are

For More Information

Books

Owen, Ruth. *Crows.* New York, NY: Windmill Books, 2012.

Pringle, Laurence. *Crows! Strange and Wonderful.* Honesdale, PA: Boyds Mills Press, 2010.

Websites

American Crow
animals.nationalgeographic.com/animals/birding/american-crow/
Read more about the American crow and find links to information about other crows.

A Murder of Crows
www.pbs.org/wnet/nature/episodes/a-murder-of-crows/introduction/5838
Watch a fascinating PBS documentary about crows and an ongoing program to study their behavior.

Index